BOLTON AS IT WAS

by

W. E. BROWN, M.A.

First edition – September 1972
Second impression – January 1973
Third impression – March 1974
Fourth impression – September 1975
Fifth impression – April 1978
Sixth impression – November 1981
Seventh impression – April 1986
Eighth impression – October 1990
Ninth impression – September 1993

Published by: Hendon Publishing Co. Ltd., Hendon Mill, Nelson, Lancashire.

Printed by Peter Fretwell & Sons Ltd., Healey Works, Goulbourne Street, Keighley, West Yorkshire BD21 1PZ.

On the cover is a reproduction of a drawing of the town centre in 1822. The market had been held here since 1251, but in 1825 it was moved to the New Market Place, now Victoria Square.

Introduction

I OWE the possibility of presenting this selection of pictures of vanished Bolton to the kind cooperation of the Chief Librarian, the Director of the Museum, and the Editor of the Bolton Evening News, who have freely lent the photographs and other pictures that I have wanted. Their staffs have been most helpful, and I must mention in particular Mr. Gordon Readyhough, Librarian of the Evening News, who has helped me to pin-point fact after fact about the illustrations. Both the Library and the Museum wish to enlarge their collection of photographs of Bolton's past, and any gifts, or loans for copying, will be most gratefully received by either.

Acknowledgments are also due to the Bolton Wanderers Football Club, to Mr. H. Gilliver and to Mr. D. O'Connor for the loan of photographs.

Mr. W. E. Brown, M.A., the author of this book, was born in Yorkshire but was educated in Toronto and at Birmingham University. He came to Bolton as Senior History Master at Bolton School (the old Grammar School) in 1944. He was the editor of the historical section of Bolton Survey.

A photograph of the painting by Selim Rothwell in 1842 of the view of Bolton from the top of the newly built chimney of William Blinkhorn's chemical works near Kay Street (later Dobson & Barlow's—see p.22) 366 feet high and the highest in England. The churches are almost in the fields—the Parish Church in the left centre, St. George's to the right, and Trinity Church in the centre background.

The natural place to begin our perambulation of the past and gone Bolton is at the medieval parish church of St. Peter. This picture was taken in 1868, when the rails had already been laid for the trucks which were to carry away its stones after it was demolished. Samuel Crompton's tomb is prominent among the already flattened tombstones of the churchyard. He was duly honoured only after his death.

The interior of the old parish church, with the galleries installed in the eighteenth century to meet the needs of a growing population. The decorated tracery of the east window is particularly fine.

The church during demolition in 1868. The works foreman stands in the west doorway beside one of the clock faces removed from the tower.

These buildings were in the immediate neighbourhood of the parish church. Opposite is the Bull & Wharf Inn at the canal terminus, where packet boats discharged passengers from Manchester in the days before railways. The inn was a late Georgian building demolished in 1966 in preparation for St. Peter's Way. Above is old St. Peter's, the parish church, during demolition in 1868.

The Church Institute was built in 1855 on land adjoining the churchyard. Its name was changed to Canon Slade Grammar School in honour of its founder, the most notable Vicar of Bolton, and it moved to its new building on Bradshaw Brow in 1956. The old school was recently demolished.

Cromwell's government took action to get this school built in accordance with the will of Robert Lever of Darcy Lever, a merchant in London who died in 1644. Bolton Grammar School, founded in 1524, moved into this building in 1658. Behind is the new parish church being built in 1870.

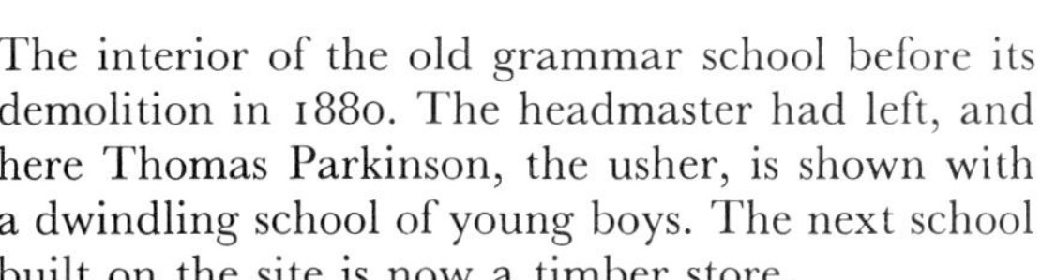

The interior of the old grammar school before its demolition in 1880. The headmaster had left, and here Thomas Parkinson, the usher, is shown with a dwindling school of young boys. The next school built on the site is now a timber store.

On our way to Nelson Square we visit Silverwell House, a country house in town before the Drill Hall was built on to this garden front. It was built by Major Pilkington in the 1790's, and here was held the famous tea party which resulted in a charter of incorporation for Bolton in 1838. It was the first independent home of the Girls' High School in 1880-1.

Our oldest photograph, showing the assembly in Nelson Square in September 1862 for the unveiling of the statue of Samuel Crompton. The policeman in front is a fine figure in his top hat. The speakers stood on the temporary balcony above the porch of the Infirmary.

Nelson Square in Edwardian times, when it still contained some dignified private houses. The clothes of the boys and girls are interesting, and here is the traditional Lancashire woman with shawl and clogs. The Infirmary had become the Education Offices, now alas soon to be pulled down.

The corner of Nelson Square and Bradshawgate in about 1902, when the Pack Horse Hotel was still a very modest little tavern. The electric trams had begun to run in 1900.

Bradshawgate looking towards the old town centre, beflagged for Queen Victoria's Jubilee in 1887. The Ship Inn, kept by Sarah Crowther, is on the left. The Chaplinesque figure in the middle of the horse-tram tracks is typical of the stunted working population of industrial Lancashire.

The old town centre, Preston's corner before Preston's. Where the market cross had stood (see cover) was a magnificent gas lamp standard. The pattern of the setts is striking. The picture must have been taken before 1880, as there are no tram tracks.

An Exact Representation of the Execution of James Earl of Derby at Bolton 1651.

A drawing of one of the most startling events in the history of Bolton, the execution, at the market cross, of James Earl of Derby in 1651. It was the sequel to Prince Rupert's massacre of the Puritan townsfolk in 1644, wrongly blamed on Lord Derby. This very imaginative reconstruction of the event first appeared in a book in 1785.

Looking back along Churchgate in 1887, with a battlemented arch to celebrate Victoria's Jubilee. There are banners of the Hearts of Oak Lodge on the left and the Sons of Izaak Walton on the right, and a fine array of cabs and cabbies. On the right are the Star Hotel, famous for what we should call cabaret shows; the Theatre Royal, whose proprietor Mr. Elliston had put up the arch; and the Victoria Theatre of Varieties, later the Grand.

The Man & Scythe in Churchgate, where Lord Derby spent his last hours and where they still have the chair in which he is believed to have sat. This photograph of 1887 again reveals in the figures of the men the grimness of Victorian Bolton. There were few women about in the streets.

Churchgate twenty years later—the cabmen's shelter was replaced by the present cross in 1909. The bow-fronted Swan Hotel had not yet acquired the corner shop (Hope Brothers). Traffic is thinly represented by bicycles, a heavy dray and a cab, and the streets are safe for pedestrians. The tramways were electrified in 1900.

Deansgate in 1887 with flags for the Jubilee. Whitehead's first shop on the corner of Crown Street is on the right, with the Bank of Bolton (now Barclay's Bank) and the turret of Williams Deacon's Bank showing further on.

Looking back along Deansgate from the corner of Knowsley Street, just before 1900, when the horse trams still flourished. The high building on the left is Williams Deacon's Bank.

Just off Deansgate in Mealhouse Lane stood the warehouse of Henry Whitehurst & Sons, corn merchants, built in 1792, and a fine example, with its hoist, of the warehouses which were once common in the town centre. The firm moved to Crown Street in 1911. Marks & Spencers now occupy the whole of this block.

An 1822 print to advertise the opening of Constantine's very modern drapery shop on Woolworth's corner. Britannia and the Lion are a splendid surprise, and with the turret and flagstaff give quite an air to the noble-fronted building next door. It is hard to believe that this, as the directories tell us, was merely the place of business of James Black, boot and shoe maker.

The top of Bridge Street in 1891. Constantine's shop had added a storey and incorporated the building next door, from which the lion had vanished but Britannia had been removed to look down on Deansgate. A pottery shop (see enlargement) occupied a part of a fine Georgian town house which had been the home of the Mechanics' Institute from 1838 to 1855. The gig, the lamp and the cobbles add to a pleasant scene.

BOLTON NEW MARKET HALL.

In the mid 19th century the Town Council, inspired by T. L. Rushton, showed a pioneering spirit. They cleared slum courts going down to the Croal, made a new high level crossing of the river in Knowsley Street, and built the Market Hall, all classical dignity outside and engineering beauty within. It was opened in 1855, and is by no means obsolete as a shopping centre today.

The interior of the Market Hall as it appeared originally, before the stalls gave place to shops in 1938.

On the other side of Knowsley Street from the Market Hall, crowded slums were to be found well into the 20th Century. On the way to the Town Hall one could diverge into little streets such as Ridgway Fold opposite. This is probably a late Victorian photograph.

Another slum in this area, Edge's Court off Central Street, photographed in 1919. On the left are two typical handloom weavers' cottages, with the loomshop in the cellar and steps up to the front door. When hand looms disappeared, these cellars became separate dwellings, the worst slums of all, until a public campaign brought about their closure.

We arrive in the new town centre, the Town Hall Square, for the centenary celebration service of the Nonconformist Sunday Schools in 1880. The importance of Sunday Schools had been educational as well as religious. Most adult Boltonians who could read had learned in these schools. Dobson & Barlow's chimney is seen in the rear, the tower of the Gas Office on the right, and the Commercial Hotel, the oldest building in the Square, on the left.

The Town Hall, built between 1867 and 1873, is here shown decorated for the Diamond Jubilee in 1897. A Farnworth horse tram stands in front, and James Lever & Son's wholesale grocery is advertising the son's already world-famous product. The fine gas lamp standard, designed by Benjamin Hick, was set up in the New Market Place in 1825. Fairy lights were used for the first time in these celebrations.

Two later ceremonies in Victoria Square. First is the visit of Andrew Carnegie in September 1910 to open three branch libraries which he had given to the town, at Great Lever, Astley Bridge and Halliwell. On the right with the moustache is the famous Chief Librarian Archibald Sparke.

In 1913 King George V and Queen Mary visited Bolton on their Lancashire tour, to unveil a memorial to Edward VII and to open the Nurses' Home of the Royal Infirmary.

The motor age has arrived. This looks like a large party assembling for a charabanc trip, but apparently, according to a complaint of the shopkeepers to the Watch Committee in 1922, it was the usual practice in the summer to pack the square with charabancs picking up their passengers. In July of that year this was forbidden.

A strange survival in present-day Bolton is Back Cheapside, a back street full of small businesses leading out of Victoria Square. This is a photograph of Back Cheapside in the late 1890's. Walter Parkinson combined the making and repairing of umbrellas with hairdressing; his main entrance was round the corner in Exchange Street. There are other local instances of this combination of occupations.

Looking back towards the Town Hall from the Great Moor Street corner of Newport Street, early in the 20th Century. Note the open top tram.

Just south of the Town Hall and behind Newport Street was Coronation Street, and here was the humble fire station of the town between 1871 and 1899. The front of Houghton's boot and shoe shop was in Newport Street.

Also south of the Town Hall, on the site now occupied by the Octagon Theatre and a car park, was the Wholesale Fruit and Vegetable Market, a retail market on Saturdays, when this picture must have been taken.

Slums adjoined Victoria Square until comparatively recently. The Eagle & Child stood in Manchester Court, Spring Gardens, and Mr. and Mrs. Wood kept it between 1898 and 1900. Note the gas pipes running up the outside walls, and the graffiti.

The Town Hall Tavern and these former weavers' cottages stood in the square behind the Town Hall until they were demolished in 1925. The well worn steps were scoured by proud housewives.

On the site of the Moor Lane Bus Station was the Bessemer Steel Works, here shown being demolished in 1927. It stood on the site of the first engineering works in Bolton, the Union Foundry of Rothwell and Hick. Behind is the gas works.

These air photographs were taken by a determinedly anonymous photographer from a Sopwith monoplane travelling at 80 miles an hour, this one in about 1928. Slum clearance has begun behind the Town Hall, the fair has moved from the Wholesale Market to its Moor Lane site. The former railway sheds seen at the corner of Deansgate and Moor Lane, mark the original terminus of the Bolton and Leigh Railway, the second in the world.

A photograph of about 1934. The Town Hall extension was nearly finished, and one half of the Civic Centre, containing the court and the police headquarters, was almost ready for occupation. The cenotaph had been placed in Victoria Square. A good view of the Georgian Commercial Hotel, now condemned to death.

With this scene, typical of industrial Lancashire, we leave the town centre. This is a view of School Hill taken from above Queen's Park. The Crofters Hotel and Union Mill stand out prominently. Many of these terraces are now demolished and replaced by modern housing, and much more will disappear in the next few years.

In 1887 an attempt was made to break a prolonged engineering strike by introducing blacklegs, and this led to serious riots. 130 Hussars arrived to keep order, and camped at Spa Road Recreation Ground.

To celebrate the Diamond Jubilee in 1897 the school children of Bolton were assembled in Spa Road Recreation Ground; these are two views of this event. Bandmaster Range in a sort of improvised pulpit is conducting massed bands and the children in a patriotic concert. The slopes of Queen's Park were full of spectators. Note the number of chimneys now demolished.

This was the British School on the corner of All Saints Street and Clarence Street, the first purpose-built elementary school in Bolton, put up by Nonconformists in 1835 to provide undenominational education. They handed it over to the Bolton School Board in 1870, when the fascia was altered. The school was replaced in 1887 on the same site by Clarence Street Board School, now the Women's Institute.

A revivalist preacher attracted a large audience at the corner of Kay Street and Turton Street in the late 1880's. Open air religious meetings were a great feature of Victorian life. This preacher's unconventional light trousers imply that he may be one of the many American revivalists who toured England. The original Falcon Inn stands on the corner.

The Park View Inn, Tonge Fold—otherwise the Dug un Kennel, Tum Fowt, celebrated in Teddy Ashton's dialect writings, as it was before 1906. It was the scene of remarkable ceremonies, some recalling heathen fertility rites, on Oak Apple Day, when a wooden bust of Charlie, looking more like an Aztec god, was placed on a table in the bar.

A hundred years ago there were many farms in what is now inner Bolton. One such was Burnden Fold, on the site of Bolton Wanderers. football ground. The club moved there in 1894.

Bolton Wanderers, one of the founder members of the Football League, had a fine team in the 1920's, when they won the F.A. Cup three times. Here is the 1926 cup-winning side at Wembley, being introduced to George V after their victory over Manchester City. The players visible are R. Pimm the goalkeeper, R. Haworth, H. Greenhalgh, J. Seddon, W. Jennings, W. Butler and J. R. Smith.

In September 1916, when only London was protected from airship raids, a Zeppelin dropped 21 bombs on Bolton, all in the area of crowded terraced houses built for handloom weavers at the foot of Deane Road, a site now mostly covered by the Institute of Technology. Kirk Street suffered the worst damage and 13 people were killed. This is a less damaged street.

In outer Bolton only a few particularly interesting sites can be noticed. Approaching Darcy Lever off Radcliffe Road is St. Stephen's and All Martyrs, a terra cotta church. John Fletcher provided the material from his Ladyshore colliery and employed John Sharpe as his architect. Unfortunately the terra cotta became porous and unreliable, and the beautiful spire, as well as the adjoining vicarage and school, have had to be demolished.

A late Victorian photograph of Hag End Brow, Lever Bridge. A typical industrial village in a river valley, where water power originally drove the machinery, dramatically highlighted by the railway bridge. Radcliffe Road continues up the opposite slope into Darcy Lever.

To the right is the old manor house of Darcy Lever, built by a branch of the Lever family in the early 17th century, and for long a farmhouse before it was demolished in 1950.

To the left Hacken Hall, Darcy Lever, built in about 1640 by the Cromptons, who combined landowning with trade. When the house was demolished in 1917 there were found, stuffed behind the panelling a piece of cotton cloth and some accounts of 1607-10 mentioning cotton wool, the earliest known reference in this country.

Great Lever Hall (left) was the home of the Levers until 1466, when it descended to the Assheton family. They sold the manor and hall in 1629 to Bishop Bridgeman of Chester, who also owned a quarter of the manor of Bolton, The Bridgemans, now represented by the Earl of Bradford, are still the greatest landowners in Bolton. The hall was demolished in 1907, and the site is now a road junction.

Just outside Bolton, but closely connected with the town's affairs, lived the Bradshaws of Bradshaw, a very ancient family who built this stone hall in the early 17th century. John Bradshaw was the officer who commanded the Parliamentary forces of Bolton in the Civil War. In the 19th century the Hardcastles, who had a bleachworks on the brook below, lived in the hall.

The finest halls in the district, Smithills, Turton Tower, and Hall i'th'Wood, have all been restored and preserved.

This aerial photograph of 1927 shows Ainsworth's bleachworks near Barrow Bridge, a fine example of industry in a rural setting. Ainsworths may well have been the oldest bleaching firm in England, well established on the Moss—now Moss Bank Park—in the early 18th century, and among the pioneers of chemical bleaching. The Ainsworths bought Smithills Hall and its estate and built Moss Bank House.

At Barrow Bridge Gardner & Bazley's Dean Mills employed 1000 people in the 1850's, supported a model village, and partly inspired the account of Millbank, the last word in progress, in Disraeli's novel 'Coningsby'. Their derelict state prior to demolition in 1913 was due to a chancery lawsuit which had forced their closure in 1877, and the failure of an attempt to revive them.

The last remains of the mill was this fine arch belonging to the engine house, demolished to allow a turn-round for the buses in 1934. The bus is one of the first in Bolton, a Leyland put in service in 1923.

Prince Albert visited Barrow Bridge in 1851 and admired its modernity, the model dwellings and the institute for the workpeople. The 'Illustrated London News' then published some illustrations, including this one of the doubling room, said to be the largest in England.

Bolton transport in different periods has had a fair showing in these pictures, with one or two exceptions. Horse omnibuses flourished from the 1860's onwards, and the one on the right is a Horwich bus outside the Beehive Hotel at Lostock in the 1890's. The man standing beside the conductor was Ben Stott.
Below on the left a private party organized by Mr. Bromilow going in his coach to Brindle point-to-point races in 1906. On the right one of the first motorbuses, with solid tyres, travelling to Lowther Street in Great Lever.

This photograph taken on the steps of The Pike on 27 August 1887 gives visual expression to the civic pride of Victorian Bolton. John Heywood (clean-shaven, back row) the owner, had given the land for a branch library in High Street, and this is his luncheon party before the stone-laying. On the right of the Mayor, Alderman Thomas Fletcher, is the Town Clerk R. G. Hinnell, on his left in front J. K. Waite, the Chief Librarian.